The

Hannah Khali

Hans Christian Andersen

methuen | drama

LONDON • NEW YORK • OXFORD • NEW DELHI • SYDNEY

METHUEN DRAMA
Bloomsbury Publishing Plc
50 Bedford Square, London, WC1B 3DP, UK
1385 Broadway, New York, NY 10018, USA
29 Earlsfort Terrace, Dublin 2, Ireland

BLOOMSBURY, METHUEN DRAMA and the Methuen
Drama logo are trademarks of Bloomsbury Publishing Plc

First published in Great Britain 2021

A catalogue record for this book is available from the British Library.

Library of Congress Control Number: 2021951479

ISBN: PB: 978-1-3503-2753-5
ePDF: 978-1-3503-2754-2
eBook: 978-1-3503-2755-9

Series: Plays for Young People

Typeset by Mark Heslington Ltd, Scarborough, North Yorkshire

To find out more about our authors and books visit
www.bloomsbury.com and sign up for our newsletters.

The Fir Tree
By Hannah Khalil

THE COMPANY

Actors	Anna Crichlow
	Bettrys Jones
	Richard Katz
	Tom Stuart
Storyteller	Paul Ready
Musical Director	Jeremy Avis
Musicians	Richie Hart
	Victoria Couper
	Natalie Lindi

PRODUCTION

Carpenters	Brendan McSherry
Casting	Becky Paris
Company Manager	Marion Marrs
Composer	James Maloney
Costume Supervisor	Mel Brookes
Deputy Stage Manager	Alannagh Cooke
Designer	Sam Wilde
Director	Michelle Terry
Globe Associate – Movement	Glynn McDonald
Head of Voice	Tess Dignan
Producer	Ellie James
Production Managers	Fay Powell-Thomas and Wills
Props Manager	Emma Hughes
Props and Puppet Makers	Katy Brooks
	Melanie Brooks
	Aimee Bygraves
	Sam Wilde
Scenic Artist	Emily Carne
Stage Manager	Rob Walker
Voice	Emma Woodvine
Wardrobe Assistant	Ruby Antonowicz Behnan

Author's Note

I have to thank the team at the Globe for this beautiful opportunity to fulfil two ambitions: to write a stage play for young people and to have a production in the wooden O. Deep gratitude to Michelle Terry and Jessica Lusk for their faith and belief in me as a writer. Also to Sam Wilde for being a dream designer and living up to his title of the 'Card Bard'. I must also thank my two in-house dramaturgs, Chris and Muna, for reading all the drafts and helping me solve the problem of death on stage. Also for teaching me about nightingales and nature and making me stop and listen.

The Fir Tree

*To the youngest dramaturg I ever worked with, my Muna.
Thank you for your insightful notes, your storyteller's
brain and your big, kind heart. I love you.*

Characters

Actor One
Actor Two
Actor Three
Actor Four
Fir Tree
Hare
Child
Stork
Sparrow One
Sparrow Two
Sparrow Three
Daddy
Girl
Cat
Guests
Mouse One
Mouse Two
Rat

There are four actors and they play all the roles. Ideally the **Storyteller** *is played by someone who is not in the main company. This could be a different person each performance.*

Part One

The Woods

The company enter singing 'Silent Night' – it continues under . . .

Four people enter the space with lanterns. They are looking for something and they've found it. A clearing with a beautiful **Fir Tree** *in the middle. Perhaps* **Actor One** *has a map.*

Actor Two   Where are we?

Actor One   Exactly where we want to be – here! This is it – this is the place.

Actor Three   Are you sure?

Actor One   Absolutely – you come through a thick huddled mass of trees, branches and leaves pressing and pushing like they don't want you to find this special place: lofty cedars, grained ash, the cloven pine, sharp hawthorn and Jove's stout oak open up into this hallowed clearing, where the wind struggles to reach but the sun shines down and warms a magic patch of earth.

Actor Four   I suppose it is quite nice . . .

Actor Two   Why are we here?

Actor One   Listen carefully and the trees will tell you.

Actor Three   Trees can't talk!

Actor One   That's not true – have you ever walked through a wood and stopped and listened to the leaves whispering to each other?

Actor Three   That's just the wind.

Actor One   Are you sure? Listen . . . now in the shade of this glade I want to tell you a story about a very special tree. A very talkative tree. A tree with dreams.

Actor Two (*pointing to an audience member*)   Is it that one there? That looks like a lovely tree. Nice branches!

Actor One   Not that one – no. The tree I want to tell you about is a Fir Tree. *This* very tree.

Actor Two   So that's why we're here!

Actor Three   Ohh tell us!

Actor Two   Is it a sad tale? I heard a sad tale's best for winter.

Actor Four   What a load of nonsense! Sadness in winter? *No*, we need hope and joy and –

Actor One   Besides . . . it's not winter.

Actor Two   It's not?

Actor Four   No, it's not. It's spring.

Actor Three   Well, someone needs to tell the weather that!

Actor One   Use your imagination – we can make spring! Come on!

They all join in, except **Actor Three** *who is sceptical.*

This is like an incantation or a spell – to conjure the season. They don't know if it will work. It's choric – like a round.

Actors One, Two and Four
   The seasons alter
   Seasons the alter
   The alter seasons
   Alter the seasons

Nothing happens.

Actor Four   It didn't work!

Actor One   It needs to be all of us – we need to work together – believe – (*to* **Actor Three**) come on.

They drag **Actor Three** *to join in and try again.*

All
> The seasons alter
> Seasons the alter
> The alter seasons
> Alter the seasons

It works. Magic.

The season changes.

Actor Three   It worked!

The company don rain macs and open umbrellas – then put their hands out to check to see if it is raining . . . general unsureness about the weather, as spring dictates . . .

Spring

Actor One   Spring! Do you see?

Actor Four   See the buds on the trees.

Actor One   Bluebells poking their heads up through the ground – making a sea of the forest floor.

Actor Four   Showers and clouds around.

Actor One   Hear the chirps of baby wrens in the nests?

Actor Four   And their mother's alarm calls when they sense the carnivorous corvids wheeling round.

Actor One   Parents protect their new-borns everywhere. On the ground and in the air. New life abounds.

Actor Four   And there's this little –

Fir Tree   Little?

Actor One   Little Fir Tree.

Fir Tree   I'm not little.

Actor Four   It doesn't like being called little.

Fir Tree   I'm not little. Why does everyone keep calling me little? I know the other trees around me are bigger than me but that doesn't make me little!

Actor One   Of course not. (*To audience.*) Just don't mention the Hare.

Actor Four   What's a hare?

Actor One   A sort of bigger boxier rabbit. And the thing you need to know about hares is that they *spring* in any season . . . here Hare comes now! Always in a hurry

Actor Four   Always late – late –

Actors One and Four   late for an important date

Hare   Oh, good morning, Fir Tree!

Fir Tree   Don't!

Hare   Sorry – do you mind if I?

Fir Tree   Don't!

Hare   I'm late again you see!

Fir Tree   PLEASE DON'T!

*We watch the **Hare** jump over the tree and speed off.*

Actor Four   And Hare did what he did every morning. He jumped over the Fir Tree – and the Fir Tree was not happy. Because nothing makes you feel quite so small as being jumped over by a hare.

Fir Tree   Every morning. Why does Hare have to do that every morning?

Actor Four   But Hare wasn't the Fir Tree's only company . . . there were children too . . .

Actor One (*as young* **Child**)   Morning, Fir Tree – do you mind if I sit here next to you and read this book?

S/he has a book which says on the cover 'The Stories of Hans Christian Anderson'.

Fir Tree   Sure.

*The **Child** begins to read, engrossed.*

A beat.

Fir Tree   What's a book?

*The **Child** looks up slightly annoyed – they were getting into their story.*

Child   This – this is a book.

Fir Tree   Oh. Right.

*The **Child** returns to reading.*

A beat.

Fir Tree   What's it for?

*The **Child** looks up slightly more annoyed – they were getting into their story.*

Child   Reading. Obviously.

Fir Tree   I see.

*The **Child** waits a moment to see if the **Fir Tree** has any further questions then, when none emerge, returns to reading.*

A beat.

Fir Tree   And what exactly is reading?

*The **Child** sighs and puts their book aside – they are clearly not going to get any reading done with this inquisitive tree.*

Child   Well, it's sort of magic.

Fir Tree   Magic? How – what does it do? Can it make a hare disappear?

Child   Oh no, not that kind of magic.

Fir Tree   Shame.

Child   It can transport you.

Fir Tree   Like the trucks that sometimes come to the forest?

Child   Um – noo – I don't think so . . . you see this book can take you anywhere, any time. It can magic you out of this wood to anywhere you like. Without ever moving.

Fir Tree   Oh how wonderful! Where does that book go?

Child   To the palace of a great Emperor in China who falls in love with a Nightingale's song!

Fir Tree   You're so lucky! Where do you get such a thing? And what is it made of?

Child   Well, a story is made of thoughts and ideas and hopes and dreams . . . and those are put into words – lots of words placed together in interesting ways.

Fir Tree   I see.

Child   And there's usually a moral.

Fir Tree   What's that?

Child   A sort of meaning or lesson, something you can learn about the world or yourself.

Fir Tree   You're very clever. And this book – what is it made of?

Child   Pages that are bound together.

Fir Tree   And pages – what are they made of?

Child   Oh. Um, pages are . . .

A beat.

Actor Four   But the child didn't have the heart to tell the curious Fir Tree that the pages of books are made from trees . . . trees that have been cut down . . .

Child   I'm – um – I'm not sure what pages are made from . . .

A beat.

Fir Tree   Well, I think books sound brilliant. I'm sick of being stuck in this boring old wood.

Child   What do you mean? It's beautiful here. Bluebells. And bees. Ladybirds and leaves.

Fir Tree   If you like that sort of thing. But it's always the same: a circle of branches, 360 degrees of soil, sky above, ground below and – I want adventure.

I want to know what the other trees know.
Go where the other trees go.
Where do they go?

A bell rings in the distance.

Child   Crickey – I'm late. Again. I'll get into such trouble! Goodbye, Fir Tree – see you another day!

Actor Four   And off the child went to school and left the tree thinking and wondering and dreaming.

Fir Tree
I want to know what the other trees know.
Go where the other trees go.
Where do they go?

Actor One   The Fir Tree was determined to find out.

Actor Four
And spring came and went
The seasons moved along as they do

The company conjure the new season with the same round as before, hesitantly at first but with growing confidence.

All
The seasons alter
Seasons the alter
The alter seasons
Alter the seasons

The company don sunhats and sunglasses, and the **Fir Tree** *grows.*

Summer

Actor One   Summer! And there are new sights and sounds in the woods.

Actor Four   The bluebells disappear and make way for daisies.

Actor One   Such a clever flower –

Actor Four   Why are they clever?

Actor One   They only grow in sunny spots. So sit with them when you're having a picnic. They're called daisies because they are the day's eye – their petals close at night as though they are asleep, then open up with the day –

Actor Four   The day's eye – I get it!

Actor One   And the children wear shorts and hats and their mums force sun cream on them.

We watch this happen.

Actor One   And the Fir Tree has grown.

Fir Tree   But not enough –

The **Hare** *appears.*

Hare   Good morning! Do you mind if I just –

The **Hare** *jumps over the tree.*

Fir Tree   Because he can still do *that*.

Hare   Have a nice day!

He disappears in a flash of tail.

Actor Four   And there were new visitors to the woods – like – the Stork.

The **Stork** *appears.*

Actor One   And when the Fir Tree saw the Stork it got excited. It knew the Stork was only visiting and with those beautiful wings of hers she could travel far and wide. She would know things. So when the Stork settles in the branches of a nearby pine, the Fir Tree calls to the Stork.

Fir Tree   Stork! Stork! Welcome back!

Actor Four   And the Stork turns a shrewd eye on the not-as-small-as-it-was Fir Tree.

Stork   My, my – haven't you grown!

Fir Tree   NO! Well, not enough anyway. But never mind that – I need your help!

Stork   Yes?

Fir Tree
I want to know what the other trees know.
Go where the other trees go.
Where do they go?
Do you know?

Stork   Oh yes. I do –

Fir Tree   Then tell me!

Stork   Are you sure you want to know? Aren't you happy here warming yourself in the sunlight and having birds nest in your boughs. Daisies at your roots and children in your –

Fir Tree   The wood is boring. I want adventure. Tell me, tell me.

Stork   Very well.

The **Stork** *flies over the audience, perhaps even landing on someone's shoulder.*

I have flown over a great city with a winding river and buildings of glass that blaze in the sunlight and there are people – so many people.

Fir Tree   Yes, yes?

Stork   And they walk beside the river and they talk and then they enter a building, a great building – a wooden O – and they stand and sit and they smile and cry as words are spoken in this round place.

Fir Tree   Words? Like the words that make stories?

Stork   Exactly.

Fir Tree   A child once told me about words and pages and books and stories . . . but what's that got to do with trees?

Stork   There are trees there too. In this round place. In fact, trees made it.

Fir Tree   Made it?

Stork   Oh yes! An army of a thousand oaks! Can you imagine the space a thousand oaks would take up – that's a whole forest! The timber frame we are in right now is made entirely from English oak – *Quercus robur* – it was made with green oak which is very young but gets stronger as it is seasoned over years so the building gets stronger with age. The largest single timber here is up there, it's thirteen-and-a-half metres long – it's literally a whole piece of tree and these two stage posts are each a timber column – whole tree pieces, this one from Norfolk and this one all the way from Scotland – they're eight-and-a-half metres each –

Fir Tree   You are very clever aren't you? And what's this place called?

Stork   A theatre.

Fir Tree   So a theatre is like a book – full of stories.

Stork   Indeed.

Fir Tree   And the trees built it themselves and now they get to hear the words and stories and laugh and cry too – and shake their leaves and branches.

Actor Four   But the Stork didn't have the heart to tell the tree that its brothers and sisters had not actually built the theatre, but that they had been cut down to make it from their wood – so she didn't answer.

A beat.

Fir Tree   What lucky fir trees. I hope one day I get to hear words spoken in a theatre and laugh and cry with the other trees.

Stork   I didn't say it was fir trees – it's the job of the mighty oaks.

Fir Tree   What about the fir trees? Where do they go?

Stork   Stop worrying about the future. You should enjoy now – warming yourself in the sunlight and having birds nest in your boughs.

Actor One   And off the Stork flew. And the Fir Tree dreamt of making a theatre like the mighty oaks and its curiosity grew –

Fir Tree   If the oak makes a theatre what does a Fir Tree do?

Actor Four   And the tree wondered and wondered and wished and wished that it would grow and that it could know what the other bigger fir trees must know.

Fir Tree   If I was taller I'd be able to see over the whole forest – maybe then I'd know . . .

Actor One   It spent so long wondering and wishing that it didn't notice the seasons moving on again. And autumn arriving in her brown coat.

The company conjure the new season with the same round as before, confidently and joyously.

All
    The seasons alter
    Seasons the alter
    The alter seasons
    Alter the seasons

The company don welly boots and scarfs and throw some dried leaves over the audience. And the **Fir Tree** *grows.*

Autumn

Actor One   Autumn. And the woods are looking different.

Some of the other trees' leaves change colour and fall from branches.

Actor Four   Like the goddess beech – the queen of the trees, whose bark was once sliced thinly and bound together to make the first books. Her leaves turn from verdant green to copper, like so many of her brothers and sisters.

Actor One   Not the Fir Tree's though because it's an evergreen.

Fir Tree   What's evergreen?

Actor Four   You, you're evergreen, you don't change colour you stay green for ever: evergreen. That's why you're a Christmas tree.

Fir Tree   A what?

Actor Four   A Christmas tree – Oh, you wait, Christmas is the best.

Actor Four *takes out a phone and plays 'Rockin' Around the Christmas Tree' loud and tinny.*

Actor One   STOP, it's not even December yet!

Actor Four   Sorry – I just get excited about . . . Alright alright – back to autumn.

Actor One   Thank you – the children come with their scarfs and Wellington boots

They kick up all the leaves that are carpeting the clearing

Gather conkers and fight to the death.

Actor Four   And the squirrels busily jump from tree
to tree.

A squirrel jumps on **Actor Four** *or on an audience member.*

Foraging for nuts.

To cheekily bury – and find again later. Buried treasure for
winter. A present . . .

Actor One   And humans forage for the beautiful
mushrooms and toadstools that cover the forest floor . . .

Stork   Sorry to stick my beak in – but the relationship
between fungi and trees is fascinating . . . really special. I'm
not just talking about the mushrooms you can see growing
on trees, but underground fungi connect different trees'
roots – helping them to talk to one another –

Actor One   That's all very interesting but we do need to get
on. And shouldn't you have migrated by now?

Stork   Well, yes I'm just going.

Actor Four   Where you off to?

Stork   Morocco. I'm taking the western migratory route –
crossing from Dover to Calais, then over the Alps and the
western Mediterranean to Rabat, the capital of Morocco.

Actor Four   Oh, I bet it's lovely there this time of year.

Actor One   Can we get on?

Actor Four   Sorry – safe journey, Stork.

The **Stork** *departs.*

Actor Four   Where was I? Oh yes. Autumn and the Fir Tree
had definitely grown.

Fir Tree   But not enough –

The **Hare** *appears.*

Hare   Good morning! Do you mind if I just –

*The **Hare** jumps over the tree.*

Fir Tree   Because he can still do *that* – he's such a show-off.

Hare   I'm not. (*A beat.*) But I can run up to forty-five miles an hour and jump about two-and-a-half metres – that's eight human feet . . . if I want to. And I want to. So – have a nice day!

He disappears in a flash of tail.

Actor One   But the Fir Tree didn't get as annoyed as it usually did. Nor did it notice the changes around it. As far as it was concerned everything was still the same.

Fir Tree   A circle of branches, 360 degrees of soil, sky above, ground below.

Actor One   It was still dreaming – dreaming of

Fir Tree
knowing what the other trees know.
Going where the other trees go.
Where do they go?

Actor Four   And before the tree knew it, it was winter.

The company cast the spell.

All
The seasons alter
Seasons the alter
The alter seasons
Alter the seasons

*The company don mittens, woolly hats and winter coats. And the **Fir Tree** grows.*

Winter

Actor One   Winter. And there are new sights and sounds in the woods. The trees have lost their leaves, all but the evergreens, and the ground is a glimmering white.

Actor Four   Shhh not so loud – remember the hedgehogs and dormice are sleeping.

Actor One   Sorry – and in the bright snow there are tracks – lorries – and men . . . busy men.

Actor Four   The children don't come as much because it is too cold.

Actor One   And the Fir Tree has grown even more because one morning . . . something is different.

The **Hare** *appears.*

Hare   Good morning! Do you mind if I just –

The **Hare** *goes to jump over the tree – but stops –*

He takes a longer run-up and goes again but stops – he can't quite make it.

Actor One   Today the Hare *could not* jump over the tree.

The **Hare** *runs around the tree having a crisis of confidence.*

Hare   Come on, old legs – we're supposed to be able to jump two-and-a-half metres . . . what's up with you? – oh (*to* **Fir Tree**, *but glummer than usual*) have a nice day . . .

He disappears in a flash of tail.

Fir Tree   NICE? NICE! PING MY PINE CONES! IT'S THE BEST DAY EVER. BECAUSE I'M NOT LITTLE ANYMORE!

Actor Four   And the tree called to the passing sparrows.

Fir Tree   Sparrows – hey! Did you see that? The Hare had to run around me – I'm too big for him to jump over me now. I'm not little any more!

Sparrow One   Oh.

Sparrow Two   Oh, oh.

Sparrow Three   That's nice, oh.

All Sparrows   But we've got to go!

Fir Tree   Where are you off to?

Sparrow One   Oh, anywhere but here.

Sparrow Two   Oh, haven't you heard.

Sparrow Three   The lumberjacks are near.

Fir Tree   Who are the lumberjacks?

Sparrow One   Oh, listen.

Sparrow Two   Hear that sound.

Sparrow One   Like a woodpecker.

Sparrow Three   But closer to the ground.

Sparrow One   And louder.

Sparrow Two   Harder.

Sparrow One   Faster.

Sparrow Three   Listen.

We hear the thud, thud, thud of a tree being cut down.

All Sparrows   They're taking down the evergreens.

It's that time of year again it seems.

Fir Tree
   I want to know what the other trees know.
   Go where the other trees go.
   Where do they go?
   Do you know?

Sparrows   Oh we know! We know! But we are afraid – we have to go

Fir Tree   Please – tell me – please!

Sparrows   Well – we'll be quick!

Sparrow One   The tree is placed in the centre of the room – a big room – a warm room – with a fireplace and –

Sparrow Two   And then it is dressed.

Fir Tree   Dressed?

Sparrow One   Like a queen.

Sparrow Three   Beautiful lights.

Sparrow One   And coloured ribbons

Sparrow Two   And underneath a carpet of

Sparrow One   PRESENTS

Sparrow Three   AND ON TOP

All Sparrows   A STAR!

Fir Tree   A star! How exciting! Then what happens next?

Sparrow One   Stop dreaming about the future. You should enjoy now – the gentle winter sunlight and snow on your boughs.

Fir Tree   But to be dressed up like a queen and everyone think you are lovely! Kept and made to feel special for ever and ever and ever and ever . . .

A beat.

Actor Four   But the Sparrows didn't have the heart to tell the Fir Tree that Christmas trees are only for Christmas, not for ever . . . so they didn't answer.

A beat.

Fir Tree   I wish it was me.

The distant sound of a bell ringing.

Sparrow Two   You may get your wish sooner than you think.

Sparrow Three   Oh, they're coming.

Sparrow One   Lumberjacks.

Sparrow Two   With their axe.

Sparrow One   Let's go.

*The **Sparrows** fly off.*

Actor One   The Fir Tree saw the gleam of steel and began to quiver from its bark to its roots.

And as the lumberjack raised his arm . . .

Actor Four   Hold on hold on a minute . . . You said this wasn't a sad tale. That's what you said.

Actor One   I know what I said and it's not. You have to see it through to the end and you'll understand – trust me.

A beat.

Now where was I – oh yes . . . As the lumberjack raised his arm . . .

Actor Four   I can't watch this lovely tree being cut down.

Actor One   Then look away.

Actor Four   And there's all these children here. They'll have nightmares – we don't want any nightmares before Christmas, thank you.

Actor One   Then they can look away too.

Actor Four   But they won't, will they? Will you?

Wait for an answer.

Oh, they're saying that now but it's like saying to someone, 'Don't think about a camel in a Christmas hat'. What are you thinking about?

Actor One   A camel in a Christmas hat.

Actor Four   See.

Actor One   Well, what do you suggest then?

Actor Four   That we skip it.

Actor One   We can't skip it – because stories are not about lying to people or pretending things are never hard or painful – because they are. We need the dark to really see the light.

Actor Four   Oh, fine go on then, I don't suppose trees feel pain anyway do they? They are inanimate objects.

Fir Tree   Who you calling an inanimate object? (*A beat.*) What is an inanimate object anyway?

Stork   Forgive me for sticking my beak in – but you are wrong . . . in fact scientists have proved that trees have emotions, they can feel pain and they like to stand close together . . . they love company.

Fir Tree   I suppose I do . . . I never really thought about it before . . .

Actor Four (*to* **Stork**)   Aren't you supposed to be in Morocco?

Actor One   Let the tree tell us tell us what happened.

Fir Tree   It was like this.

The **Fir Tree** *leads, but the company all do the actions of the felling of the tree, the swinging of the axe, and the creaking and falling – they should use their voices; it shouldn't be tuneful but should be loud and expressive. Instruments can also be used. Their bodies all become the falling tree.*

We hear the axe thud, thud, thud (this can be vocal or a banging)

an in-breath

thud, thud, thud

A harder, higher sharper in-breath

Thud

Creak

Fall

Big sigh (this should be deep, asthmatic, raspy – a death rattle).

Actor One   The axe cut deep.

Actor Two   The tree fell with a sigh.

Actor One   It felt faint, sore – but the not-so-little Fir Tree got its wish at last.

Actor Four   It was going to go where the other trees go.

The company quietly sing/hum in the background 'In the Bleak Midwinter' behind this next part.

In the bleak midwinter
Frosty wind made moan
Earth stood hard as iron
Water like a stone
Snow had fallen
Snow on snow on snow
In the bleak midwinter
Long, long ago

Angels and Arc Angels
May have travelled there
Cherubim and Seraphim
Thronged the air
But only his Mother
In her maiden bliss
Worshipped the beloved
With a kiss

What can I give him?
Poor as I am
If I were a shepherd
I would give a lamb
If I were a wise man
I would do my part
But what I can I give him
Give him my heart
Give him my heart

Actor One   But adventures aren't all fun and games, you know. Not at all. Sometimes they can be scary – taking a risk – doing something new . . . and the Fir Tree definitely trembled a bit as it was taken from its home in the woods, and loaded on to the back of a van. The sparrows and the Hare came out to wave it goodbye and the spot where it had stood for all those seasons looked very empty and sad.

The song ends.

Fir Tree
I've changed my mind
I don't want to know what the other trees know
go where the other trees go
Away through the snow
Into the unknown . . .
I'll miss my . . .

Actor Four   But it was too late –

Fir Tree   home

Actor Four   the adventure had already begun . . .

Fir Tree
Grabbing me,
dragging me,
wrapping me,
pushing me.

Actor Four   Into the van it went

Fir Tree
So many bright lights
Wheels
So many
Hard wind – harder than I've known
A sharp strong metal smell in the air
Up and down
this way and that
until

Actor One   suddenly the truck

STOPPED.

Everyone looks around in anticipation.

We are at the tree sale.

Fir Tree   And there are other trees everywhere. Trees like me. A forest. But a forest . . . without . . . roots.

Daddy   Which one do you like?

Actor One   And a little girl was peering at the tree and saying

Girl   This one, Daddy, I want this beautiful tree!

Daddy   Isn't it a bit . . .

Fir Tree   Don't say little . . .

Daddy   – little?

Fir Tree   I'm not little!

Girl   Not to me – it's perfect!

Fir Tree   She thinks I'm perfect!

Actor One   And the tree felt happier – it would all be OK.

Daddy   Well, if you're sure, I mean there are lots of people waiting to buy trees here – it is Christmas Eve after all . . .

Girl   I'm sure, this is the tree for me.

Daddy   Not that one over there?

Girl   No this is the perfect fir tree.

Fir Tree   She thinks I'm perfect! But she can't hear me . . . why can't she hear me?

Actor Four   And then there were hands again.

All
  Grabbing the tree,
  dragging the tree,
  pushing the tree,

pulling the tree,
propping the tree
unceremoniously
until it was back upright again –

Actor Four   but *inside*

Fir Tree   That's better – oh and look where I am! The Sparrows were right! A big room – warm – with a fireplace – oh, it is quite hot – hotter than summer . . . I can feel my needles crisping a bit but it is beautiful, I can get used to the heat and how nice to have a different view at last! Who needs a forest when you can have a glass square to look though onto a – road? But what is that great wooden thing? (*It means the piano.*) That's the funniest looking tree I've ever seen – hello? Hello? (*No answer.*) Fine. Suit yourself if you don't want to chat . . . The little girl talked to me . . . But why couldn't she hear me?

The **Cat** *Ophelia is scrapping playfully with a low branch.*

Fir Tree   Hey – stop that! Leave me alone.

Cat   Spoilsport!

Fir Tree   You can hear me! But the little girl couldn't . . .

Cat   You really are green aren't you?

Fir Tree   Green? Of course I'm a tree!

Cat   No. It means you don't know much.

Fir Tree   Well, there's no need to be rude. (*A beat.*) If you tell me why she couldn't hear me you can play with my branches . . .

Cat   Isn't it obvious? It's because you've been cut down. You've lost your voice. But I *can* hear you because I'm more-than human.

Fir Tree   More-than human?

Cat   Yup. Humans have the ability to hear nature but they don't listen. Only a few use that power. And yet, they all think they're better than animals, nature – but they're not. We see things they don't, understand the world better. So we are *more-than humans* – get it?

Fir Tree   I see. And once a tree has been cut down only more-than humans can hear us . . . Oh. I didn't know that would happen . . . Well. I must try and be positive. This is a lovely new home after all . . . And I'm still keen to know what happens next . . . Now what did the Sparrows say? Can you remember?

All   DECORATING TIME!

Boxes appear with decorations inside.

Girl   Where is it? Where is it?

Daddy   What are you looking for, darling?

Girl   My favourite decoration – it's in here somewhere!

Daddy *produces a gaudy bauble.*

Daddy   Is it this one?

Girl   No!

A beat.

Daddy   What about?

He produces an even gaudier bauble.

Girl   No, no!

Daddy   Then it must be –

The most foul ostentatious thing is in his hand.

Girl   NO – here it is!

She holds a regular pine cone aloft.

Daddy   Really? That's your favourite? That sad little pine cone.

Girl   It's not sad, it's special – I found it in the woods. I was reading under a tree and it just dropped right into my lap. It was like a present: so perfectly formed, so beautiful – a present from nature, look at it. Don't you remember – you said I should spray it gold but I said no, I like it better this way, and of all the decorations it's the one that looks like it belongs on the tree most, because it does!

The **Girl** *puts it on the tree.*

Daddy   And are we allowed to put other decorations on as well?

Girl   Of course! Come on!

Everyone decorates the **Fir Tree** *while an upbeat Christmas pop tune ('Rockin' Around the Christmas Tree', ideally) blares from speakers.*

Once the **Fir Tree** *is ready:*

Girl   There – even more perfect.

Daddy   You were absolutely right about this tree. It looks beautiful. There's just one thing missing.

Girl   Presents underneath, ribbons on its branches, pine cone in place and lights . . . what else? (*To the audience.*) Do you know?

She listens for an answer from the audience.

Of course – the *star*. Where can it be?

> Twinkle, twinkle, little star
> How I wonder where you are?

Looks in anticipation.

No sign of it – Daddy, will you help?

They try together.

> Twinkle, twinkle, little star
> How we wonder where you are?

Nothing. Maybe you all should do it? Just you lot, really, really imagine the star, and sing with all your heart.

Twinkle, twinkle, little star
How we wonder where you are?

The star floats down from the sky and is attached to the top of the **Fir Tree***.*

Is it there? You did it! Thank you so much for your help!

Actor One   And the tree caught a glimpse of itself in the mirror and couldn't believe it!

Fir Tree
Is that really me?
Little me?
It can't be!
So sparkly!

Daddy   The tree really is perfect now.

They all admire it.

Actor One   And now it was late and the Fir Tree was feeling pretty shaky. After the journey in the truck and then the moving and the decorating – and the heat of the room – it was rather overwhelmed. And it trembled to its branches, knocking off several decorations. Ophelia the Cat got blamed and was very grumpy about it.

Girl   Go on, shoo – we can't have you ruining our beautiful tree while we are all in bed.

The **Cat** *blows a raspberry and grumps off.*

Girl   Good night, tree.

Off they go to bed.

Fir Tree   Oh, what a day I've had. Everything the Sparrows said came true. The room. The decorating. And here I am in the dark. Everyone is upstairs asleep. But I can't rest. I can't sleep. I'm too excited . . . what will tomorrow bring? I want to know what happens next . . .

A beat.

Girl   CHRISTMAS DAY!

Daddy   No – no – it's not morning yet it's still dark!

Girl   Come on, Daddy, up you get! Good morning, tree.
HAPPY CHRISTMAS!

Fir Tree   She's so excited! Opening presents and, oh, now
there are lots of people – sparkly jumpers, red lips, smiles,
food in mouth, gulping, laughing and –

Guest   Such a lovely tree.

Guest   I've always adored their wallpaper.

Guest   What's the secret ingredient?

Guest   Don't put that down there.

Guest   It's been such a strange time . . .

Guest   No more chocolate for you!

Guest   Say thank you to Granny!

Guest   We've just been so busy.

Guest   Where did you get it?

Actor One   But the tree didn't hear all this – it was still
wondering what came next.

The company sing 'O Christmas Tree' under.

Fir Tree   I want to know what the other trees know.

Actor One   It barely even heard the song being sung in its
honour.

The company continue to sing 'O Christmas Tree':

O Christmas Tree, O Christmas Tree,
How lovely are your branches!
O Christmas Tree, O Christmas Tree,
How lovely are your branches!
Not only green in summer's heat,
But also winter's snow and sleet.
O Christmas Tree, O Christmas Tree,
How lovely are your branches!

O Christmas Tree, O Christmas Tree,
Of all the trees most lovely;
O Christmas Tree, O Christmas Tree,
Of all the trees most lovely.
Each year you bring to us delight
With brightly shining Christmas light!
O Christmas Tree, O Christmas Tree,
Of all the trees most lovely.

O Christmas Tree, O Christmas Tree,
We learn from all your beauty;
O Christmas Tree, O Christmas Tree,
We learn from all your beauty.
Your bright green leaves with festive cheer,
Give hope and strength throughout the year.
O Christmas Tree, O Christmas Tree,
We learn from all your beauty.

*The is a loud banging on the door that interrupts the end of the
song. Everyone stops and turns.*

Part Two

The Nightingale

Daddy   Who could that be? On Christmas Day. Uninvited.

Girl   Open it and see.

Daddy   No. Everyone we know is here. Let's just ignore it.

Girl   Daddy! It's very cold outside, you can't leave someone out there – I'll answer it.

She goes to the door and the cloaked **Storyteller** *enters the room.*

Girl   We have a guest – they've offered us a story in return for a warm drink and a few minutes out of the cold. What do you all think? Would you all like a story?

Wait for a response.

Let's settle down with some hot chocolate.

Daddy   Or mulled wine. Help yourselves. Please sit down.

A grand **Storyteller***'s chair is pulled into the space.*

The **Storyteller** *has a book. It is the same book of Hans Christian Andersen stories that the* **Child** *had at the start.*

Fir Tree   They have a book – full of pages – and stories . . .

Storyteller   Hello everyone. Thank you for welcoming me so kindly.

Girl   Hello, Storyteller – where are we going today?

Storyteller   This book has a story that will take us to China.

Fir Tree   China!

Daddy   Right, everyone settle down nice and cosy and listen.

Storyteller   The story is called 'The Nightingale' . . . so we fly to the court of a great Emperor. This Emperor had the most beautiful palace and gardens that would make you gasp to see. And if you ever had the energy to walk all the way through them, because they covered miles and miles, when you came to the final flower bed and walked through the final hedge you would find a small wood next to a lake. In that wood lived a Nightingale, and the Nightingale had the sweetest song ears have ever heard.

One day a lady who was writing a book about China ventured as far as the wood and was treated to the Nightingale's song. She was amazed by its beauty and when she wrote her book, she described the wonders of the palace, the colours of the gardens, the height of the hedges, but she finished by saying the jewel in the crown of the Emperor's kingdom was the Nightingale that sang in the woods by the lake.

Now the writer of the book sent a copy to the Emperor, who read it with great interest: he was delighted at the praise she heaped upon his luxurious palace, he was charmed by her descriptions of the technicolour gardens, but when he reached the part about the Nightingale his smile turned to a frown and he called his courtiers to him: 'What is this Nightingale I'm reading about – why have I never heard it sing?' The courtiers all looked confused – they had never walked the length of the gardens on their lazy little legs and so had never been anywhere near the wood. When they looked blank the Emperor demanded they go and find the Nightingale and bring it to the court that very evening. Terrified of the Emperor's displeasure the courtiers got in a flap, running up and down the stairs, looking out of windows, trying to find the Nightingale. They asked the servants in the palace who mostly shrugged their shoulders, but one young girl who worked in the kitchens said that she had indeed heard the Nightingale, because she had to walk through the little wood on her way home. She said when she heard it singing it made her cry because it was like being kissed by her grandmother. The courtiers begged the girl to show them the bird. So she agreed and led them out into the gardens. They huffed and puffed past the regiments of roses, the legions of lavender, the battalions of begonia, until they reached the wood. There they sat and waited, desperate to hear this special song.

They waited and waited.

And then at last they heard a moo-ving sound.

*The **Actors** moo.*

And the courtiers looked at one another and smiled and said, 'Is that it? Is that the beautiful song of the Nightingale?'

'No,' said the kitchen girl, 'that is just the cows lowing in the field.'

The courtiers were disappointed and becoming impatient but they sat a little longer and now came a riveting sound.

*The **Actors** croak like frogs.*

And the courtiers looked at one another and smiled and said, 'Is that it? Is that the beautiful song of the Nightingale?'

'No,' said the kitchen girl, 'that is a family of frogs.'

The courtiers were now very disappointed and impatient and becoming terrified that they would have to return to the Emperor without the Nightingale, when suddenly the most beautiful sound split the silence.

We hear the song of the Nightingale.

And the courtiers did not need to ask the question – they knew exactly what the beautiful sound was. It brought tears to their eyes. When the Nightingale drew breath the courtiers applauded and the bird was very surprised – he wasn't used to an audience. The courtiers then begged him to come and sing for the Emperor that evening in the palace: 'But my song sounds better in the green wood,' he replied. The courtiers, however, insisted, and the gracious Nightingale agreed.

That night, the Emperor himself had the chance to hear this rare bird sing. The Nightingale flew into the centre of the court and sang his little heart out, and everyone gasped and tears rolled from their eyes. When the Nightingale finished there was thunderous applause. And the Emperor himself was wiping his eyes. The Nightingale was pleased; if he could make an Emperor cry he must have a very fine song indeed, he thought. And so the Emperor declared the Nightingale his most treasured possession and had a golden cage built for him. He was allowed to leave the palace three times a day, but had delicate silver threads attached to his wings so he could never go too far, and he would sing for the Emperor whenever he asked. And everyone knew about this Nightingale; people would come from far and wide to hear him sing, they would buy Nightingale paintings for their houses, wear clothes embroidered with the Nightingale's image and sing songs inspired by his tunes. The Nightingale was famous. But he wasn't happy.

Then one day a gift arrived at the palace for the Emperor who opened it to discover that a very clever clockmaker had designed a clockwork nightingale! It was made of beautiful precious stones and it had a little dial in its back that you could turn to make it sing. So he turned the dial and the little wind-up Nightingale sang a pretty tune – it was nothing to the sound of the real Nightingale but it pleased the Emperor, so he wound it again, and again, and the court all sighed and laughed and clapped their hands in amusement. And while they were busy watching this new trinket of the Emperor's the real Nightingale slipped out of his cage, broke his silver chains and flew away in relief.

Now when the Emperor noticed the real bird's disappearance he was cross, but only for a moment because the courtiers said what an ungrateful bird he was and how dare he leave all the luxuries of the palace. They asked, 'Why would he want to return to the woods?' and assured the Emperor saying, 'This bird is better, it's much more beautiful and never needs a rest'. And the Emperor agreed and turned the dial of the fake Nightingale once more. Every day he would keep his fake Nightingale at his side, reassured it could never fly away and leave him, and that that he could make it sing whenever he wanted.

But one day something awful happened . . . he turned the dial and a crunching noise alerted him to the fact that the bejewelled Nightingale was broken! All the clockmakers in the land were called, and they studied his trophy carefully, but no one thought they could fix it. One clockmaker, however, managed to make it work again but she warned the Emperor, saying, 'You've wound it so much all of the cogs inside are worn out, so you must only use it very, very rarely, otherwise it'll break again and then it'll be impossible to fix'. So the Emperor named a special day once a year on which he could play the bejewelled Nightingale. And the rest of the time the palace was silent of music.

Not long after this, the Emperor got very ill. Everyone was afraid he was going to die. They crept around the palace which became an even more hushed, sad place without sounds of voices or laughter or music. The whole kingdom was worried. One dark night, the sick Emperor lay on his bed looking at the bejewelled Nightingale wishing it would sing for him. Then suddenly he felt a chill pass through the room and realised he was not alone, Death was sitting on the edge of the bed looking at him. The Emperor was terrified as Death leaned over and lifted the crown from his head placing it on to his own skull. The Emperor begged Death, offering him all the jewels in the land – even his precious clockwork Nightingale – if he would spare him. Death shook his head and said, 'There is nothing you can offer me'. The Emperor thought a moment and replied: 'What about the most beautiful sound in the world – surely that would interest you?' Death looked intrigued, so the Emperor called out for the real Nightingale – who heard in the silent night and appeared at the window. When Death saw him he said, 'You're the bird with the sweetest song are you? I would like to hear you sing.'

So the Nightingale sang and Death was entranced – tears streaming down his face. And when the song was finished Death said to the Emperor: 'The beauty of the Nightingale's song has saved you – for now. But I will be back, Death comes to everyone eventually.' He then removed the Emperor's crown from his skull, returned it to its rightful owner and left the room.

The Emperor, who had been so close to Death, sat up and smiled joyfully at the Nightingale. 'You did it! You saved me with your song!' But the Nightingale looked sad: 'My song was never for you . . . do you know why the Nightingale sings?' The Emperor shook his head. 'I sing to find a mate and I have been singing and singing but have found no other like me, because in your land all the green woods have disappeared to make way for your gardens, so now I must be alone.'

The Emperor was shocked and ordered that all his gardens be allowed to grow wild, in the hope that this would help the Nightingale to find his mate one day. And as the seasons altered, the Emperor watched the grounds become more and more overgrown, and he fell in love with nature, spending more time outside the palace than in it. But he realised amongst all the beauty and wildness there was one thing missing – the Nightingale's song. It had disappeared from the land. The Emperor didn't know why the Nightingale had gone – had he at last found a mate? Or perhaps he'd flown away to a new home. The Emperor was desperate to know the end of the story. So, he sat himself on a mossy bank in the woods by a thicket and he sits there still, waiting and listening and hoping one day to hear the Nightingale's song once more . . . That, my friends, is the story of the Emperor and the Nightingale.

A round of applause.

Actor One   Now the Fir Tree for once had been listening to this story of the Nightingale.

Fir Tree   What a story! And I'm sure it has a moral. A child once told me that stories always have a moral. I must try and work out what the moral of that one is.

Actor Four   And so the story was over. And the singing was over and the evening was coming to an end. Everyone said thank you to the Storyteller and bid them goodbye.

Girl   Thank you, Storyteller! Everyone – let's say thank you, and Merry Christmas.

Storyteller   Merry Christmas!

Encourage audience to thank the **Storyteller** *as they leave.*

Actor One   And now it was very late . . .

Daddy   My goodness, is that the time? Come on, everyone, bed.

Actor One   And just like that the lights went out. And the Fir Tree was in the dark. But it was happy.

Fir Tree
Now I know what the other trees know.
And tomorrow when it starts all over again
I'll be ready and I'll enjoy it even more.

A bell rings in the distance.

The Attic

Actor One   But the next morning everything changed again.

During the next section the decorations are removed from the tree.

Actor Four   People came into the room and once again there were hands

All
Grabbing the tree,
Stripping the tree,
dragging the tree,

> pushing the tree,
> pulling the tree,
> propping the tree
> unceremoniously
> until it was upstairs.

Fir Tree   What am I doing up here?

Actor One   And the door was shut and the tree was left alone and confused in the dark attic.

Fir Tree   Maybe they keep me up here in the daytime and just bring me down at night?

Actor Four   But day turned into night and no one came.

Actor One   And night turned into day and no one came.

Actor Four   And the tree began to feel very sad and lonely. Like the Nightingale felt when he was put in a cage.

Fir Tree   Where is everybody? They can't have forgotten me can they?

Actor One   And day turned into night and the tree remembered its woodland home.

Fir Tree   I wonder if the snow is thick in the wood . . . if the hedgehogs are hibernating – their slow heartbeats pulsing through all the roots, and if Hare is leaving footprints everywhere he goes . . . I never thought I'd miss that Hare.

Actor Four   And the tree felt thoroughly miserable. And alone.

Actor One   But it wasn't.

Actor Four   Oh no – it had neighbours and didn't even know it.

Two **Mice** *appear.*

Actor One   Two mice.

Actor Four   Two curious mice.

Mouse One   Hello.

Fir Tree   Oh you gave me a surprise – I thought I was all alone.

Mouse Two   No – we are here too. Isn't it brie-zing?

Mouse One   Don't you mean freezing?

Mouse Two   That's what I said. It's cold. Don't you think so, old Fir Tree?

Fir Tree   Old? I'm not old. In the wood where I'm from other trees around me are much, much older than me!

Mouse Two   Oh you're from the wood – he's from the wood – do you know my cousin the field mouse?

Fir Tree   Oh no, I don't think I met him.

Mouse Two   I've never met him either, you see we stay inside – we are house mouses.

Mouse One   Mice.

Mouse Two   That's what I said. I'm Benedick, and this is Beatrice. There used to be brie of us.

Mouse One   Three of us.

Mouse Two   That's what I said, and our brother Will decided to go downstairs. He was very curious.

Mouse One   Always wanted to know what the other mice know.

Go where the other mice go.

Mouse Two   So he went downstairs.

Mouse One   And never came back.

Mouse Two   Do you know where the other mice go?

The **Fir Tree** *looks nervous.*

A beat.

Fir Tree   I know about the woods.

Mouse One   You do?

Fir Tree   Yes, that's where I lived before I came here.

Mice   Tell us, tell us.

Fir Tree   Well, in spring

Bluebells poke their heads up through the ground – making a sea of the forest floor

Showers and clouds around

The chirps of baby wrens in the nests.

Then in summer,

The bluebells disappear and make way for daisies

Such a clever flower – you only find them in sunny spots.

In autumn

The wood looks different

Some of the other trees' leaves change colour and fall from branches

And the squirrels busily jump from tree to tree

Foraging for nuts

To cheekily bury – and find again later. Buried treasure for winter. A present . . .

Winter.

When the ground is a glimmering white. Snow.

Mouse Two   Oh that sounds horrible. Cold!

Fir Tree   No, no, it wasn't horrible – it was lovely. Perfect.

Mouse One   Then why are you in here?

Fir Tree   I wanted to know what happened next . . .

Mice
Yes, us too!
We want to know what the other mice know.
Go where the other mice go –

Mouse Two   like Will who went downstairs and never came back – do you know what happened to him?

Actor One   But the Fir Tree didn't have the heart to tell the mice that there was a cat downstairs called Ophelia . . . and we all know what cats do to mice . . . so it didn't answer.

Fir Tree   Um . . . how about a story?

Mouse One   What's a story?

Fir Tree   Well, it's sort of magic.

Mouse Two   Magic? How – what does it do?

Fir Tree   A story can take you anywhere, any time. It can magic you out of this attic to anywhere you like. Without ever moving.

Mouse Two   Oh, how wonderful! Where does this story go?

Fir Tree   To the palace of a great Emperor in China who falls in love with a Nightingale's song!

Actor One   And so the Fir Tree told the mice the story of the Nightingale – the very same one it had heard and that you all heard. And the mice oohed.

Mice   Oooooh.

Actor One   And ahhed.

Mice   Ahhhh.

Actor One   And were completely transported from the attic for a short time – it was magic.

And they came back night after night to hear the story again and again. They didn't get bored of it. And then the next week they bought their distant relation the Rat.

Mice   This is the tree, this is the tree.

Fir Tree   Hello.

Rat   Well, hello. I'm Iago and I hear tellings that you've got a good story.

Fir Tree   Well the mice seem to like it.

Mouse One   We do.

Mouse Two   It's very Gouda.

Mouse One   You mean good.

Mouse Two   That's what I said. I like it.

Rat   Let's hear it then.

Actor One   So the Fir Tree told the story of the Emperor and the Nightingale once more and Iago the Rat listened and Benedick and Beatrice the mice watched Iago the Rat listening until the very end.

Fir Tree   And that is the story of the Emperor and the Nightingale.

A beat.

Mouse One   Well? What did you think?

Mouse Two   What did you think, Iago?

Rat   It's alright.

Fir Tree   Alright?

Rat   To be honest I'm surprised you two liked it – I thought there'd be more cheese.

Fir Tree   Cheese?

Mouse One   True – it could have a cut of camembert.

Mouse Two   A fork of feta.

Mouse One   A bite of brie.

Mouse Two   A mite of mozzarella.

Rat   Myself, I'd have liked a bit more in the kitchen section.

Fir Tree   What kitchen section?

Rat   When they go and ask the kitchen girl for help – she could have been in the middle of cutting up some bacon slices for the Emperor's breakfast, and then left them on the table in her hurry to show them the wood – just left them on the table for anyone to grab and gobble up.

Fir Tree   But that's not the point of the –

Rat   Or if she forgot to put the butter away, just left it out open in the warm kitchen where it got all melty and gooey for anyone to grab and gobble up and –

Fir Tree   I don't think you've quite understood the point of the –

Rat   Don't you reckon, you two ? Bit more cheddar, bit less chat.

Mice   Yeah. More cheddar, less chat. We thought that too.

Mouse One   I didn't think it was that good.

Mouse Two   Noo.

Rat   Needed less Nightin*gale*, more Wensley*dale*.

Fir Tree   I don't think you understood the point of the story.

Rat   What is the point of the story?

Fir Tree   Well – it's about how more-than humans, that's us, we have a job to do . . . a Nightingale's song is to find a mate.

Mouse One   What about trees – what do trees do?

Mouse Two   They look pretty for Christmas then get put in the attic.

Fir Tree   No, that's not my job at all.

Actor One   And the Fir Tree thought about how foolish it had been – to be longing for the next thing – to want to leave the wood. When it should have treasured its time there, where it belonged . . .

The attic door is flung open.

Rat and Mice   People! RUN!

They disappear.

Fir Tree   Oh, what now . . . Maybe they are taking me home – home to the wood!

Daddy   Here it is – I knew it was still up here . . .

Actor Four   And once again there were hands

All
Grabbing the tree,
dragging the tree,
pushing the tree,
pulling the tree,
unceremoniously
until it was downstairs

Actor One   and out of the front door

Girl   What are you doing with our lovely tree?

Daddy   It's not lovely any more – it's old and decrepit – look most of its needles have come off and what's left is yellow.

Fir Tree   They said I was evergreen – I'm not supposed to go yellow!

Girl   It's still beautiful to me.

Daddy   We can all appreciate its beauty when it warms the house.

Girl   Warms the house – you can't be planning to . . .! PUT DOWN THAT AXE!

Actor One   The Fir Tree saw the gleam of steel and began to quiver from its bark to its roots.

Fir Tree   Not this! Not AGAIN!

Actor One   And as the man raised his arm . . .

Girl   PLEASE – leave my tree.

Fir Tree
    Now I really know
    Know what the other trees know
    Know where they go
    and the truth fills me with *woe*

The sound of a distant bell.

Actor Four   I won't let you do this. It's awful.

Actor One   It is. But I have the power to change the story . . . we all do.

Actor Four   What do you mean?

Actor One   Let's rewind. Sprinkle a bit of Christmas magic and make the story different. Watch . . . you see I was the Child with the book. That was me. And I want to go back and do it over again. Change it . . .

They transform.

Safe Tree

Actor One (*as young* **Child**)   Morning, Fir Tree – do you mind if I sit here next to you and read this book?

Fir Tree   What's a book?

Child   This – this is a book.

Fir Tree   What's it for?

Child   Well, it's sort of magic.

Fir Tree   Magic?

Child   It can transport you.

Fir Tree   Like the trucks that sometimes come to the forest?

Child   Um – noo – I don't think so . . . you see this book can take you anywhere, any time. It can magic you out of this wood to anywhere you like. Without ever moving.

Fir Tree   Oh, how wonderful! Where does that book go?

Child   To the palace of a great Emperor in China who falls in love with a Nightingale's song!

Fir Tree   You're so lucky! Where do you get such a thing? And what is it made of?

Child   Well, the story is made of thoughts and ideas and hopes and dreams . . . and those are put into words – lots of words placed together in interesting ways.

Fir Tree   I see.

Child   And there's usually a moral.

Fir Tree   What's that?

Child   A sort of meaning or lesson, something you can learn about the world or yourself.

Fir Tree   You're very clever. And this book – what is that made of?

Child   Pages that are bound together.

Fir Tree   And pages – what are they made of?

Child   Oh. Um, pages are . . .

A beat.

Actor Four   And the child was brave and told the truth to the curious Fir Tree that the pages of books are made from trees . . . and that trees are cut down to make books and musical instruments like guitars and pianos – and to build things like theatres.

Fir Tree   What kind of trees?

Child   Oaks mainly, I think.

Fir Tree   What about fir trees?

Child   Well, they are normally cut down to be decorated as beautiful Christmas trees.

Fir Tree   Oh, I see . . . I want adventures – I want to be decorated and looked at and sung about – but I don't want to be cut down.

Actor Four   And the child thought. S/he thought about the story of the Nightingale and how the Nightingale needed to be in nature. S/he thought about what s/he'd learned at school – that trees turn carbon dioxide into the oxygen that humans breathe. How much humans *need* trees to live. And then s/he had an idea!

Child   I've got it!

Actor Four   Off s/he ran and came back with lots of people and they all had . . . spades.

The company produce spades.

The Fir Tree saw the gleam of steel but it didn't quiver from its bark to its roots. Because there was no axe. The people started digging – digging it up and putting it in a pot! And the Fir Tree spent that winter decorated and beautiful inside the house, and then the rest of the year it was taken into the garden where it enjoyed the seasons, sunlight and wind in its boughs. And it was happy.

Fir Tree   Yes, I'm happy. But I have one more question: What about the space left in the wood where I once stood – doesn't it look strange and empty?

Child   Don't worry – I thought of that too – I planted a seed that will grow into another little fir tree to take your place.

Fir Tree   Did you plant my pine cone?

Child   I thought about it – but the clever Stork told me that wouldn't work.

Stork *flies in*.

Stork   I don't mean to stick my beak in but – you can't just plant a cone . . . you have to get the seeds out of the cone – put it in a paper bag in a warm room and shake it every few days.

Child   Yes.

Stork   And then, when the cone is dry enough to release the seeds you pop them in the freezer for three months. Why?

Child   Because then the seeds think it's winter.

Stork   Exactly. Then you plant the seeds.

Child   I did it. And it worked. Thank you.

Stork   You're welcome.

A beat.

Thank you.

Child   What for?

Stork
   You saved a tree
   and planted a tree
   behaved responsibly.
   Now I'd better be off, that winter sun is calling . . .

Actor Four   So is that what really happened? You dug up the tree and put it in a bucket?

Child   Maybe. Or maybe it was cut down. Or maybe we decided not to have a tree this Christmas. Or maybe we decorated a tree in the garden. Or maybe after Christmas we sent it to a special place to be recycled naturally so it became part of the soil and the forest once more . . .

Actor Three   And maybe we decided to take Fridays off school to listen to nature, speak up for her – or to help other people hear what the trees need.

Actor Four   Are we like the Emperor then? Learning, doing better and waiting for the end of the story?

Child   We are . . .

Actor Three   S/he is clever isn't s/he, that child. Let's hope s/he grows into a clever adult. Because that's what we need. Clever, responsible grown-ups to mend the relationship between humans and more-than humans. To learn to listen to nature again.

Fir Tree   S/he is clever. Trees are clever too: Do you know what the pine tree told me? It said 'Every time you read a book a tree smiles knowing they can live for ever'. I like the idea of becoming a book one day – having a child leaf through my pages . . . but not until I'm old. For now I'm still a *little* Fir Tree and I like it.

A beat.

A bell rings.

Actor One
> To me, fair friend, you never can be old,
> For as you were when first your eye I eyed,
> Such seems your beauty still. Three winters cold
> Have from the forests shook three summers' pride,
> Three beauteous springs to yellow autumn turn'd
> In process of the seasons have I seen,
> Three April perfumes in three hot Junes burn'd,
> Since first I saw you fresh, which yet are green.

Actor Four
> And that's one ending for a special Fir Tree
> how it found adventure and safety
> thanks to a clever, kind
> and thoughtful child.

All   Merry Christmas, everyone!

The company all sing 'Rockin' Around the Christmas Tree'.

Ends.